"Grammar, like Caesar's wife, should not only be pure, but above suspicion of impurity."

"The Tes Little Book of Grammar *offers a great deal more than its modest title implies. It represents an informative, engaging and supportive arm around the shoulder of every teacher of English and literacy.*"
Mick Connell
PGCE tutor at Sheffield University and member of NATE

"This is a fab little guide. I love the 'opportunity for smugness' which enables all readers to get 'in' on the joke and move from seeing grammar as scary to being part of the grammar geek gang (which is the best gang going)."
Rebecca Foster
Head of English

"With simple explanations and humorous tips about correct usage, this will be invaluable to any primary school teacher. Not only will it help you teach well, it will ensure that you're always the most revered grammarian at the party."
Aidan Severs
Primary lead practitioner

"This essential booklet contains common-sense crib sheets that will demystify the grammar required for everything from report writing to prepping students for the Year 6 Sats or new GCSE SPaG requirements. Genuinely fantastic!"
Caroline Spalding
Assistant headteacher

The **tes** little book of

Grammar

Adi Bloom

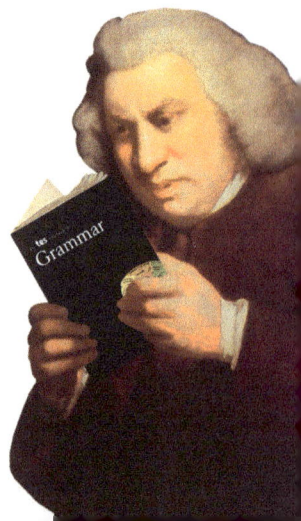

When I sat down to take the key stage 2 English grammar, punctuation and spelling sample paper not that long ago, it is safe to say that I was not-so-quietly confident.

English grammar and I go way back. I've been a journalist all my life, have edited two magazines and was once even a chief sub-editor, which meant that I spent my days shouting at other professional journalists over their misuse of the humble comma and the clauses left dangling in their articles.

Surely, a test designed for 11-year-olds would be no match for my awesome pedantic knowledge, I thought.

So confident was I that I whizzed through all the questions in just 20 minutes – less than half the time that pupils were given to complete the test – and merrily packed off my paper for external marking without a second thought.

Of course, there is always a lesson to be learned from overconfidence. My paper was returned to me with a mark of 80 per cent: hardly a score to celebrate for someone who has made a living out of her ability tell a hyphen from an en dash at 20 paces.

Unfortunately, the skill to be able to spot a mistake at a glance is what ultimately tripped me up, as I lost marks more than once for failing to "read the question properly". But that is the thing about tests. They assess your theoretical understanding of concepts, without measuring how well that understanding might be applied elsewhere.

Putting the nature of tests aside, though, the fact is: grammar is hard. Even grammar geeks like me recognise that. And teachers everywhere, many of whom are still struggling to get to grips with the grammatical requirements of the new national curriculum and exam specifications, will be nodding their heads in agreement.

Children are no longer expected to just be able to use grammar accurately, they are also required to know all the right names for things and to be able to pick them out of a line-up. Instilling this knowledge is no easy task, especially for teachers who were themselves educated under a system that took a rather more relaxed approach to grammar learning.

That's what this book is here to help with. Confident pupils require teachers who are themselves confident about the ins and outs of grammar. Having an exact definition and a few simple examples to draw upon when a pupil asks "But, Miss, what is a noun phrase?" can be a lifesaver.

However, there is another point to this book. Grammar is tough. There's no denying that. It's something that even chief sub-editors can sometimes feel unsure about. But grammar is also fascinating, intricate and, when used properly, a tool to help you create works of literary genius.

If we can remove the fear around grammar, both pupils and teachers will benefit. Hopefully, reading through the entries listed on the following pages will make everything a little less scary and demonstrate that teaching and learning about grammar really isn't pointless. I love breaking rules. But to confidently break them, you need to know what they are and how they came about. Only then will pupils be able to appreciate how, in the right hands, the humble comma can be a thing of beauty.

Ann Mroz
Editor
Tes

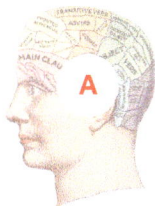

Active and passive voice

The active voice is when the subject of the sentence is doing the main verb of the sentence:

Lily is finishing her homework.

The passive voice is when something is being done to the subject of the sentence – ie, the subject itself is entirely passive.

Lily's homework is being finished.

The passive voice often leaves one particular question dangling: by whom? It is particularly useful, therefore, when discussing scary homework deadlines that you can't quite bring yourself to face:

My essay will be done in time.

It's also handy for tabloid headlines: their goal is to raise a question that can be answered only by reading the article. So:

National debt cancelled
NHS services axed
Schools to be closed

Adjective

Adjectives are words used to describe nouns. So:

My pet elephant is tall, fat and grey, and performs stunts in her spare time.

You can also create adjectives out of other parts of speech, provided that they're being used to describe a noun. As a rule, these compound adjectives need to be hyphenated, so that it's clear they're referring to the noun. So:

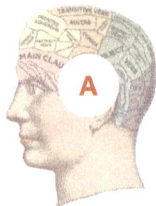

My envy-inducing birthday present is an elephant who performs death-defying stunts.

Without the hyphen, you would read the phrase "My envy" and assume that this, rather than the birthday present, was the subject of the sentence.
Be careful not to overuse adjectives, or your readers will feel as though they're having to hack their way through your prose with a machete.

My favourite pet elephant is tall, fat and grey, and performs death-defying stunts of astonishing daring in her copious spare time.

Used well, adjectives draw attention to the most important part of a sentence. So: is the point here that your pet elephant has lots of spare time? That you have more than one elephant? That she's generally elephant-like in appearance? Surely the point is simply:

My pet elephant performs death-defying stunts in her spare time.

Adjectival phrase
This is a group of words that describes the noun or pronoun in the sentence. The adjective itself can appear at the start, in the middle or at the end of the group of words.

That meal was quite edible.
That meal was edible enough.
That meal was edible enough for the price.

An adjectival phrase can also include a complement (see COMPLEMENT): that is, a phrase needed to make sense of the adjective.

She was aware (adjective) *of the danger of eating a very cheap*

meal (complement).
Are you** really willing* (modifier + adjective) *to put your health at risk in order to save a bit of money* (complement)?***

Adverb

Adverbs are used to describe the way in which a verb is being done. Very often, they end with "-ly". So:

He cried disconsolately.
She ventured forth intrepidly.
They spoke softly.
They walked on tiptoes.
I'll get out of bed soon.

But be careful: the adverb describes the way in which the person or thing doing the verb is completing that action. It does not describe the way other people feel about it.

The man sadly died.

This suggests that the man was very sad – crying, perhaps? – as he died.

He was tragically killed.

How do you kill someone tragically? Perhaps you wear a sad-face mask and clutch your chest as you do it.
Adverbs can also be used to modify – that is, to change – an adjective or another adverb.

That jungle was pretty (adverb) **scary** (adjective).
The ghost howled, slightly (adverb) **scarily** (adverb).

Adverbial phrase

Adverbial phrases are entire phrases that modify a verb,

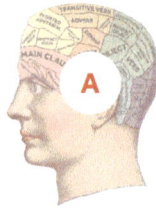

adjective or adverb. They tend to answer the questions "when?", "where?" and "how?"

We'll venture into the jungle *in the morning*.
There will be monkeys playing *in the jungle*.
So as not to scare the monkeys, we should walk *in an orderly fashion*.

Fronted adverbial

A fronted adverbial is an adverbial phrase that has been moved to the front of a sentence. It really is that simple. So:

In the morning, *we'll venture into the jungle.*
In the jungle, *we'll see monkeys playing.*
In an orderly fashion, *they marched through the trees.*

Apostrophe

An apostrophe is used either to indicate possession or to replace one or more letters that have been removed from a word.

Possessive apostrophe

The possessive apostrophe indicates when something belongs to something else. In the singular, it takes the form apostrophe then "s".

May's cuddly dog
Isaac's CD of songs from musicals

For plural words that end in an "s", the rule is simple: the apostrophe always follows the "s":

The cats' whiskers
The monkeys' bananas

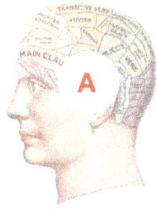

If a plural does not end in an "s" – "women"; "children" – then the apostrophe goes before the "s". Otherwise you'd be talking about the womens, which is something only Twitter trolls do.

The women's hammers
The children's toys

Singular words ending in "s" are more complicated, largely because opinion is divided. Following the same rule you would use for plurals can look neater: an apostrophe, and no additional "s". So:

Mars' orbit around the Sun
Brussels' decision to impose sanctions

But others argue that, when you pronounce the apostrophe as an additional "es" sound, it should be followed by an "s". So:

Jesus's disciples
The bus's headlights

Still others would include an "s" in all instances. Ultimately, the rule is that there is no rule: what you do is up to you. This is not something you hear often in grammar, so enjoy the freedom.

Apostrophe to indicate omission
If a letter is removed from a word, its absence is indicated using an apostrophe. So: "is not" is abbreviated to "isn't", "it is" to "it's" and "was not" to "wasn't".
Similarly – and this is where mistakes happen – "you are" is abbreviated to "you're" and "they are" to "they're". "Your" and "their" are different words entirely. See YOUR/YOU'RE and THERE/THEIR/THEY'RE.

Opportunity for smugness: look out for all those signs advertising "rock 'n roll". That "n" stands for "and", so two letters – "a" and "d" – have been removed. The correct version

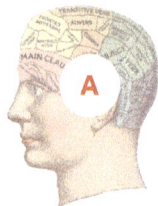

is therefore "rock 'n' roll". Because nothing says rock 'n' roll like correct grammar.

Apostrophe to indicate the plural
They don't. Not ever. No, not even in special cases. Never.

Asyndetic list

Most lists follow a basic structure. They list an item, another item, another item and a final item. (Occasionally, a list will use an alternative conjunction, such as "or" or "but not" in place of "and".) These are called syndetic lists.
An asyndetic list, however, misses out that final conjunction. So it lists an item, another item, another item, a final item. Like that.

Auxiliary verb

In some sentences, one verb will suffice. In these cases, the action is usually over fairly swiftly:

The dog barked.
The car alarm sounded.

In some sentences, however, the action continues for a length of time, requiring more than one verb:

The dog was barking all day.

There are two verbs here: the auxiliary verb – "was" – and the present participle – "barking". (See PARTICIPLE for more information on the latter.)

"To be" and "to have"
Auxiliary verbs can be any tense or conjugation of the verbs "to be" or "to have", if used in conjunction with a present or past participle:

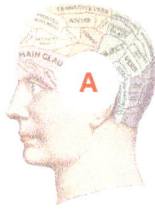

The dog was barking all day.
Was = auxiliary; barking = present participle

The car alarm has sounded on and off all day today.
Has = auxiliary; sounded = past participle

"To do"
Any tense or conjugation of the verb "to do" can also function as
an auxiliary verb, when combined with the infinitive form (with
the "to" removed) of another verb:

I do believe in Santa Claus.

Do = auxiliary; believe = main verb

It's true: you did finish your homework on time.

Did = auxiliary; finish = main verb

He will be good next year.

Will = auxiliary; be = main verb

Modal verb
Modal verbs such as "must" and "should" function as auxiliary
verbs. For more information, see MODAL VERB.

Combination
Auxiliary verbs can also be used in combination with one
another:

I must have believed in Santa Claus when I was a child.
The car alarm had been sounding all day, before I heard it.
*I should have listened to my teachers when they told me to finish
my homework.*
He will be going to the party.

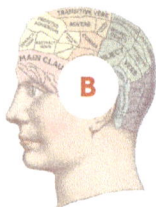

Brackets/dashes

Commas are used to separate a non-essential clause from the rest of the sentence:

The teenagers, who had been partying all night, slept all day.

However, sometimes the non-essential clause is not entirely relevant to the main purpose of the sentence. It's almost an add-on, or an afterthought. In those cases, the clause would be separated off using dashes instead:

The partying teenagers – who, as teenagers, had a general disposition towards indolence, anyway – slept all day.

And, on occasions, the non-essential clause is so irrelevant to the main purpose of the sentence that you want to tuck it away in brackets, where it won't get in anyone's way:

The partying teenagers (is there any other kind of teenager?) slept all day.

Capitalisation

First, the dos: do start a sentence with a capital letter. Do give proper nouns – such as names of people and places – capital letters. Now the don'ts: don't upgrade nouns to proper nouns for no reason. However important a job title may be, it does not take a capital letter. (This applies to any job. You are president of the US, although your personal title may be President Brown.) Similarly, don't refer to School, or Maths or Work Experience.

Opportunity for smugness: a lot of people end up very confused about whether or not to capitalise "Mum" and "Dad", but the rule is in fact very simple. If you are using "Dad" as someone's name, then it follows the rules of a name: it takes a capital letter. So: "Hey, Dad. Come over here a minute." If,

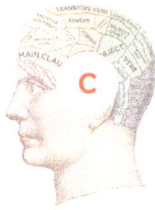

however, you are using it as a job title – "my mum" – then it follows the rule of job titles, and is not capitalised. So: "My mum did my homework for me."

Clause

A clause includes a subject and a verb. This distinguishes it from a phrase, such as a noun phrase or an adjectival phrase, which does not include both those elements.

Main clause
The main – or independent – clause can stand on its own as a full sentence. It contains a subject and a verb that together complete an action.

The clown smiled menacingly.
The elephant stood on its head.

Subordinate clause
This is also known as a dependent clause, because it cannot stand on its own – it is always dependent on the main clause. It takes the form conjunction + subject + verb. In each of the following examples, the subordinate clause is in red. The rest of the sentence is the main clause.

I grew scared whenever the clown smiled menacingly.
Because she was standing on her head, the elephant's ears turned pink.

Note that the subordinate clause can come either before or after the main clause, and is usually separated from it by a comma.

Noun clause
Any phrase that functions as a noun in a sentence, even if it does not actually include a noun, is a noun clause.

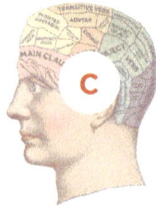

Acrobatic elephants make clowns happy.

Here, the sentence uses a conventional noun phrase: "acrobatic elephants".

It's a mystery what makes clowns happy.

In place of a noun here, we have a noun clause: "what makes clowns happy".

I can't remember my exact words (noun phrase).
I can't remember what I said last night (noun clause).
Their biggest disappointment was losing the match (noun phrase).
Their biggest disappointment was that they didn't make it to the semi-finals (noun clause).

Adjectival clause

These clauses function as adjectives in a sentence: they describe a noun. They begin with a relative pronoun – "who", "whom", "whose", "which" or "that". In the following examples, the adjectival clause is in red.

The clown, whose menacing smile scared small children, was actually just expressing happiness.
The elephant that can stand on her head is easily distinguished by her pink ears.

Some adjectival clauses are boundaried by commas – as in the first example – and some are not. If you can remove an adjectival clause from a sentence without affecting the fundamental meaning of the sentence, then you would use commas to mark it off. If – as in the second example – the sentence would make no sense at all if you removed the adjectival clause, then you should not use commas.

(For when to use "that" and when to use "which", see WHICH/ THAT.)

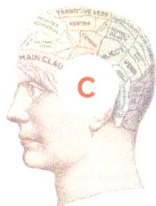

Adverbial clause

These clauses function as adverbs: they're used to describe a verb. They usually begin with words such as "when", "where", "why" or "after".

The clown was just expressing happiness when he smiled. After standing on her head for too long, the elephant saw that her ears had turned pink.

Dangling clause

These happen when the subject of a subordinate clause does not match the subject of the main clause. It's very easily done, but with unintended comic results.

Rushing to catch the bus, Hannah's teddy bear fell on the ground.

The subject of the main clause is "Hannah's teddy bear", thus suggesting that Hannah's teddy bear was rushing to catch the bus. So the sentence should be: while rushing to catch the bus, Hannah dropped her teddy bear.

While walking the dog, the tree collapsed.

Was the tree walking the dog? Better to say: while I was walking the dog, the tree collapsed.

I have some of the chocolate cake that Jonah baked in my schoolbag.

Did Jonah really bake the chocolate cake in your schoolbag? Better to say: in my schoolbag, I have some of the chocolate cake that Jonah baked.

It may help to think of the old joke: "Last night, I shot an elephant in my pyjamas. How an elephant got in my pyjamas, I will never know..."

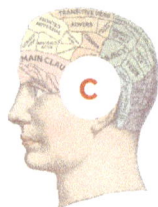

Cognate

A cognate is a word that has the same etymological origin as another word. It's unlikely you'll be expected to offer up examples without a detailed knowledge of the origin of languages, but learning about cognates can be quite fun. For example, the words "chief" and "chef" both have their root in the Middle French word "chef", meaning "head".
Cognates across languages are also interesting: the Hebrew word "shalom" (peace) shares its origin with the Arabic word "salaam", also meaning "peace". In French, one wears a chemise (shirt), and in Hindi one wears a kameez (shirt). This way language geekery lies.

Colon

A colon is used to introduce an elaboration on a theme. This sounds confusing, but it can be broken down into one of two forms.

Introducing a list
A colon in effect says, "Everything that follows me belongs to a list." For example:

My favourite punctuation marks are: semicolons, ellipses, hyphens and dashes.

Expansion
A colon can be used to expand on a statement that has come before, providing more detail. For example:

She couldn't believe what she was seeing: 12 dancing elephants, all dressed in tutus and silken veils.

Opportunity for smugness: in British English, a colon is followed by a lower-case letter. In US English, it's followed by a capital letter. Anyone British who follows a colon with a capital letter has either been reading US newspapers or learning their grammar from Twitter.

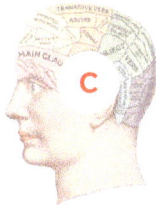

Comma

People tend to describe the comma as providing breathing space in a sentence: imagine that you're reading a sentence out loud, and need to pause for breath. And it's true that reading an overly long sentence without any commas can leave the reader feeling breathless at its end. But a comma can also be used for clarification. On the whole, commas should surround a subordinate clause, if that subordinate clause is not integral to the sentence:

This white wine, which I bought in France, is very nice.

If, however, a clause is integral to the overall context of the sentence, it should not be boundaried by commas:

The wine that I'll be serving tonight is French.

And a comma should never separate a subject from its verb:

My dog Fido, barks very loudly.

The comma after "Fido" separates it from its verb – "bark" – and is therefore wrong.

On the whole, people tend to use the comma correctly. There are, however, three commas of contention.

The Oxford comma

There are two grammatically acceptable ways of writing lists:

Today, at the shops, I plan to buy a bag of apples, a punnet of strawberries and a small mountain lion.
Today, at the shops, I plan to buy a bag of apples, a punnet of strawberries, and a small mountain lion.

The comma before the "and" in the second sentence is referred to as the Oxford comma, or serial comma. It's used primarily

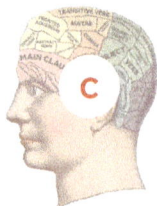

by Americans; Brits tend to eschew it. However, there are times when the Oxford comma is undoubtedly useful. Take the following examples:

This book is dedicated to my parents, Hillary Clinton and God.
We invited the strippers, JFK and Stalin.

Use of the Oxford comma in the first case would have avoided unnecessary mental images of divine copulation and/or comparisons between Bill Clinton and God. In the second example, it may well have made the party considerably less interesting, but that depends on your personal proclivities.

The only comma
This is an unofficial name for this comma, but it's a handy one: you use the only comma when you have only one of the thing that follows it. So:

She wanted to thank her father, Pop McPopson.
She fed her pet elephant, Freda.

But, if you have more than one of the thing being mentioned, using a comma can be misleading:

She invited her classmate, Maya, for dinner.

This suggests that there are only two people in the class: the "she" who is the subject of the sentence, and Maya.
Imagine, therefore, that the father-thanking, elephant-owning, classmate-hosting girl in the sentences above actually comes from a two-father family, owns a whole herd of pet elephants and has 30 people in her class. In that case, the sentences would read:

She wanted to thank her father Pop McPopson.
She fed her pet elephant Freda.
She invited her classmate Maya for dinner.

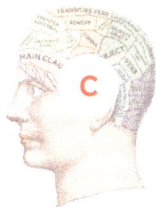

Comma splice

These are evil. This is a non-negotiable fact: comma splices are evil.

A comma splice is when a writer uses a comma in place of a full stop, to link two independent clauses. So:

She went to the North Pole on holiday, it was very cold.

Shudder. And not just because it's cold in the North Pole. This is never acceptable. Ever. There are two handy pieces of punctuation that can be used instead:

She went to the North Pole on holiday. It was very cold.
She went to the North Pole on holiday; it was very cold.

The poor comma is already overworked. Give the semicolon a chance.

Compare with/compare to

"Compare with" is used to illustrate difference. It highlights contrast. For example: "Three adults volunteered for the snowball fight, compared with the nine children who came forward."

"Compare to" is used to illustrate similarity. For example – famously – Shakespeare asked: "Shall I compare thee to a summer's day?" What he meant was: "Shall I liken you to a summer's day? Is that a good metaphor?"

Opportunity for smugness: everyone, but everyone, gets this one wrong. Really. People are constantly using "compared to" to illustrate a contrast. They are wrong.

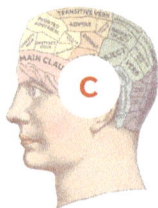

Complement

A complement gives additional information about the subject or object of a sentence. It can be a noun phrase or an adjectival phrase.

Subject complement

The subject complement is easily confused with the object of a sentence (which is a confusing sentence in itself). But, whereas the object brings a new entity into the sentence (imagine a second person appearing, with a little "ta-da!"), the subject complement simply provides you with more information about the subject of the sentence. So:

Tod has many neighbours.

Here, Tod is the subject of the sentence, and his neighbours (ta-da!) are the object.

Tod is a sardine.

Here, the word "sardine" simply tells you more about Tod. So it is the subject complement, rather than the object of the sentence.

Tod is a rare Mongolian sardine.

In this sentence, the entire noun phrase "rare Mongolian sardine" is the subject complement, because it is all there to provide more information about Tod.
Adjectival phrases can also be used as complements. So:

Tod is greasy and smelly.
Here, "greasy and smelly" is the complement (although not, it should be noted, the compliment).

Tod's neighbour tasted a bit unpleasant.

Here, "a bit unpleasant" is the complement to the subject of the sentence, which in this case is the noun phrase "Tod's neighbour".

A subordinate clause can also be used as a subject complement, as long as it provides more information about the subject. So:

The first thing I did on arrival **was check that Tod was still in his can.**

The phrase "the first thing I did on arrival" provides more information about the subject of the sentence – "I" – checking that Tod was still in his can.

Object complement

That last example actually contains two complements: a subject complement and an object complement. The object complement is in red below:

The first thing I did on arrival was check that Tod was *still in his can*.

The subject of the sentence is "I", checking on Tod. Tod, therefore, is the object of the sentence. The phrase "still in his can" – the object complement – provides the reader with more information about Tod.

So: the object complement functions in exactly the same way as the subject complement, but provides you with more information about the object of the sentence.

Complex sentence

see SENTENCE

Compound sentence

see SENTENCE

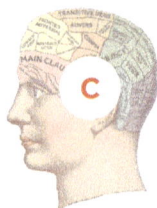

Conjugation

see VERB

Conjunction

Conjunctions link two separate clauses, within a single sentence:

I fed my pet elephant and then went to school.
I fed my pet elephant but forgot to have my own breakfast.
I forgot to have my breakfast because I was so busy feeding my pet elephant.
I was busy feeding my pet elephant, so I forgot to eat breakfast.
I love my pet elephant, although she does take up a lot of my time.

They can also link items in a list:

Do you want your chocolate cake with vanilla ice cream, hot fudge sauce or a biscuit on the side?
I'm really hungry, so I want chocolate cake and vanilla ice cream and hot fudge sauce and a biscuit on the side.

Can you start a sentence with a conjunction? Yes, you can, and don't let anyone tell you otherwise.

Although she takes up a lot of my time, I love my pet elephant.
Because I was so busy feeding my pet elephant, I forgot to have breakfast.
But don't you get hungry if you skip meals?

Dashes

see BRACKETS/DASHES

Definite article

see DETERMINER

D

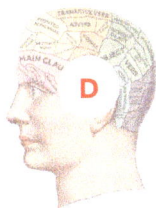

Demonstrative

see DETERMINER

Determiner

Determiners are words placed in front of a noun, to clarify what the nouns refer to. They are divided into several categories.

Definite article
The name here is a helpful clue: the definite article is what you use when you are definitely referring to one particular article. Specifically, it is the word "the". So:

This is the dance I was telling you about.

Indefinite article
Again, the name is helpful: you are referring to one of a particular type of object, but you can't be more definite than that. Specifically, indefinite articles are the words "a" and "an". So:

It's a dance – one of those ones where you move your arms and legs at the same time.

Demonstrative
These are used to demonstrate which object you are talking about. Demonstratives are the words "this", "that", "these" and "those". So:

See those people moving their arms and legs at the same time? That's the dance I told you about.

General determiner
Imagine waving your hands vaguely when you talk about these words. They are words to use when you're a little hazy about the detail: "a few", "a little", "a lot of", "any", "another", "enough",

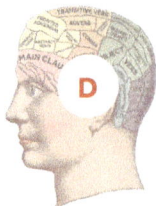

"many", "most", "much", "other", "quite", "some", "such" and "what". So:

No, that's not my dance. That's another dance. You can't point to any group of people moving their arms and legs and assume it's my dance. There are such a lot of dances out there.

Number
These are easy: you already know what numbers are. So:

My dance is only one of many. In my social circle alone, we've invented about 20 dances.

Possessive determiner
These determine to whom the object being discussed belongs. They are the words "my", "your", "his", "her", "its", "our" and "their". So:

See that group over there? They're doing my dance.

Direct object

see OBJECT

Ellipsis

Ellipses are used to indicate information being left out of a sentence.
They can be handy when quoting extracts from a speech or book:
Mark Antony said, "Friends, Romans...lend me your ears."

They can also be used when leaving a thought unfinished:
Mark Antony said, "Friends, Romans, countrymen, lend me..."

Note: one set of three dots is an ellipsis. More than one set are ellipses.

E

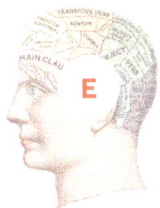

Exclamation mark

An exclamation mark is used to indicate an exclamatory remark. Are your eyes widening and your hands flapping when you say something? Are you bouncing in your seat with enthusiasm? In that case, an exclamation mark is called for. So: "Hurrah!" or "Congratulations!" or "Happy birthday!" If you are not a hand-wavy, seat-bouncy kind of person, you would be entirely within your rights to deadpan "Hurrah", "Congratulations" or "Happy birthday".

Fronted adverbial

see ADVERB

Full stop

A full stop is the punctuation mark that comes at the end of a sentence. Like that. In the US, it's known as a period, which is why US TV programmes often feature actors saying, "I'm not doing that. Period."

General determiner

see DETERMINER

Gerund

A gerund is a verb that has become a noun. This sounds complicated but is actually very simple: it's done by adding "–ing" to the end of a verb, creating a present participle (see PARTICIPLE) that can double as a noun. People use some gerunds all the time, without even realising it. For example: "the comings and goings" or "the goings on". (You know a word is a noun if you can put "the" in front of it.)
But there are others, too:

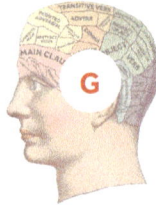

He listened to the sound of her breathing.
The parsing of a sentence is easy.

But be aware that because a gerund is a noun, it takes the possessive pronoun. For example:

She listened to the sound of his walking up and down.
He'd had enough of Micha's clowning around.

Most people would be tempted to write:

She listened to the sound of him walking up and down.
He'd had enough of Micha clowning around.

But that doesn't work with a noun. You wouldn't, for example, say:

She listened as he went for him daily walk up and down the street.

Instead, you'd use the possessive: "his daily walk". So, too, "his walking up and down".

Homophone

Homophones are words that sound the same, but have different meanings. Some examples:

New/knew
Discrete/discreet
Loan/lone

Opportunity for smugness: look out for signs offering a "sneak peak". A peak is a mountain summit; a peek is a glance. So, rather than offering you a sneak glance at something, these signs are offering you a covert mountain top.

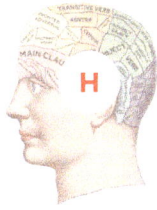

Hyphen

Hyphens are used to join together separate words into a single phrase. Most commonly, this is used to turn two separate words into a single adjective with a different meaning. Take, for example, the local authority that advertised the fact that it had "over 60 play areas". Phrased that way, it indicates that the borough is endowed with a large number of play areas. However, had it been written "over-60 play areas", it would have indicated that the borough has thoughtfully introduced play areas for its pensioners.

Imperative verb

Imperative verbs are used to give an order:

It is imperative that you listen and obey.

Even when followed by a (potentially passive-aggressive) "please", they leave little room for discussion. If you can plausibly follow a verb with "or else", then it's likely to be an imperative. So:

*Wash up **after yourself.*** (Or else I'll be very cross.)
*Do **your homework.*** (Or else I'll be very cross.)
Please** do **your homework. (Or else you'll fail your exams.)
*I'm begging you: do **your homework, please.*** (Or else I'll tear out my own hair.)
*Don't touch **that.*** (Or else you'll break it, and then you'll have to pay for it.)
Push. (Or else you'll be stuck outside for all eternity.)

Indefinite article

see DETERMINER

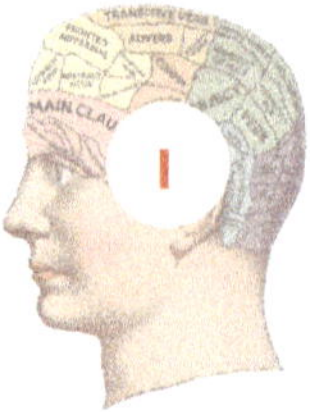

Indirect object

see OBJECT

Infinitive

see VERB

Intransitive verb

see VERB

Inverted commas

Also known as quotation marks or speech marks, inverted commas are used to quote a piece of speech, or an extract of someone else's writing.

There are very clear stylistic rules around using inverted commas. If you're quoting either a full sentence of writing, or a piece of speech, the quotation is preceded by a colon or a comma. (On the whole, the rule tends to be that journalists use colons, while novelists use commas.) Whatever is within quotation marks starts with a capital letter. The punctuation at the end of the extract or piece of speech is enclosed inside the quotation marks. For example:

The Tes Little Book of Grammar *says: "Inverted commas are used to quote a piece of speech, or an extract of someone else's writing."*

Inverted commas can also be used to quote fragments of writing or of speech. For example:

The Tes Little Book of Grammar *says that the stylistic rules around using inverted commas are "very clear".*

When the phrase inside quotation marks is not a full sentence, it does not require a preceding colon or comma, or an opening capital letter. It forms part of a larger sentence – rather than a

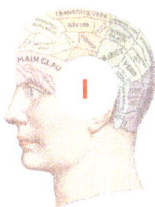

sentence of its own – and so any punctuation falls outside the quotation marks, as part of the broader sentence.

Only opinions – so, in the example above, what *The Tes Little Book of Grammar* thinks about stylistic rules – should be enclosed in quotation marks. Many people find it tempting to write something like this:

The Tes Little Book of Grammar *says that the "stylistic rules" around using inverted commas are "very clear".*

While "stylistic rules" has been quoted from *The Tes Little Book of Grammar*, it is not an opinion, so there is no reason to place it in quotation marks. If you don't like that particular phrasing, simply rephrase it in a way you prefer:

The Tes Little Book of Grammar *says that the way to style inverted commas is "very clear".*

In fact, placing phrases that are not opinion into quotation marks makes you sound sarcastic:

"Well, Tes *says that they're stylistic rules, but I don't believe it. Personally, I think it's a grammatical free-for-all."*

Less/fewer

A remarkable number of people use "less" and "fewer" incorrectly, given how simple the rule really is.

"Fewer" is used when you are referring to something that you can count:

I have fewer biscuits than you do.

"Less" is used when you are referring to something you cannot count:

I have less tea than you do.

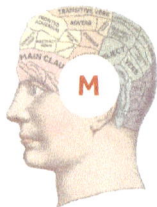

Modal verb

A modal verb indicates necessity, possibility or probability. This sounds as though it covers pretty much all eventualities, but it becomes much clearer when one lists the modal verbs:

Can
Could
May
Might
Must
Shall
Should
Will
Would

Modal verbs are used to discuss ability:

She really can touch her toes with her nose.

They are used to ask permission:

Please may I try to touch my toes with my nose? (Or, more archaically: *might I try to touch my toes with my nose?*)

And they are used to make requests and offers:

Would you like me to teach you to touch your toes with your nose? I'm sure I could do it.

Neither/nobody/no one

These words always take the singular verb. So: *"No one is available"*, *"Neither of them is right"*, etc. Not a lot of people know this rule, and so you'll see the incorrect version – *"Neither of them are right"* – in print all the time. The easiest way to remember the rule might be to think of "no one" as an

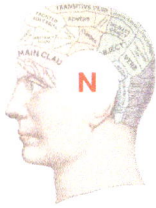

abbreviation of "not one" and "nobody" as an abbreviation of "not one body". So: "Not one of them is right".

None

"None", while an abbreviation of "not one", can take either the singular or the plural form. So: *"Elephants are very good dancers, but none of them have won* **Strictly.** *"* Or: *"Elephants are very good dancers, but none of them has won* **Strictly.** *"*

Noun

A noun denotes a person, object, place or thing. Here's a fail-safe test: if you can put "the" before a word, then it is a noun. So "the person", "the stone", "the hill", "the terror" are all nouns. "The ungrammatically" or "the thinks" are not nouns.

Proper noun
A proper noun is the name of something, usually a person or a place. A proper noun always takes a capital letter.

The girl in the Superman T-shirt is called Grace.
Saul is travelling to India with British Airways.

Concrete noun
A concrete noun is something physical: it is something you can observe or touch or otherwise experience with your senses. Like concrete. Proper nouns can also be concrete nouns.

In India, Saul will visit temples, monasteries and museums.
In the temples, he may be invited to light incense as an offering to the gods.

Abstract noun
An abstract noun is something intangible: you cannot experience it with your senses. They tend to be emotions,

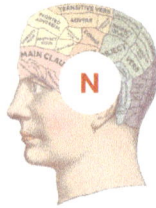

ideas, concepts or states of being.

Good friendships, like good relationships, should be full of love. The US Declaration of Independence calls for life, liberty and the pursuit of happiness.

(In any other context, "declaration" and "independence" would also be abstract nouns. But the US Declaration of Independence is a written document, and therefore a concrete noun.)

Compound noun

A compound noun is a new noun, made up of two pre-existing words that have been combined to create a new word. Neither of these pre-existing words has to be a noun.

Policeman (noun + noun)
Haircut (noun + verb)
Passerby (noun + preposition)
Drycleaning (adjective + gerund)
Greenhouse (adjective + noun)
Overthrow (preposition + verb)
Declaration of Independence (noun + preposition + noun)

Noun phrase

A noun phrase is made up of a noun, plus the words that are used to describe it. For example, imagine that the word "elephant" appears in a sentence. But you own a whole herd of elephants, so you need more help to distinguish which elephant the sentence is referring to. The noun phrase contains anything that will help in this task.

That elephant
Aunt Agatha's favourite elephant
The elephant on the sofa
The elephant wearing a wig
The angry-looking elephant

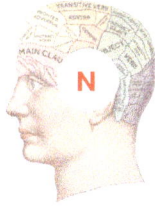

Number/amount

This follows the same rule as LESS/FEWER: you have a number of something you can count, but an amount of something you can't count. So:

I have less sugar than you, but fewer sugar lumps.
I have an amount of sugar, but a number of sugar lumps.

Number

see DETERMINER

Object

The object is the secondary noun in a sentence.
The subject of a sentence is the noun doing the main action (or, in the case of a passive sentence, having the main action done to it). In the sentence "Kabir is writing", for example, Kabir is the subject.
However, you can elaborate on that sentence by adding additional nouns: "Kabir is writing a postcard", for example, or "Kabir is writing to his pet elephant." Those additional nouns are the objects of the sentence.
There are two types of objects: direct and indirect objects.

Direct object
Direct objects answer the question "what?" or "whom?"

Kabir is writing a postcard.
The question is "what is Kabir writing?" The answer is the direct object: the postcard.

Indirect object
An indirect object answers the question "to whom?", "for whom?" or "for what?"

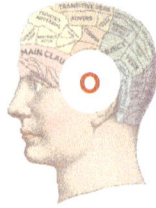

Kabir is writing his pet elephant a postcard.

The question is "to whom is Kabir writing a postcard?" The answer is the indirect object: his pet elephant.

Object complement

see COMPLEMENT

Only comma

see COMMA

Oxford comma

see COMMA

Parsing

To parse a sentence is to break a sentence down into its constituent grammatical parts. Like taking apart a car engine and laying out all the pieces of machinery. Only less messy, and with less risk of explosion.

Participle

There are two types of participle of a verb: present participle and past participle. The present participle always takes the same form: verb + ing. So: "laughing", "crying", "conjugating". The past participle is more complicated. Often, it takes the form verb + ed: "laughed", "cried", "conjugated". Sometimes, though, it is an entirely new form: "rung", "sung", "swum", "lay". There's no handy way to learn these: it's simply a case of memorising them. Participles play three different roles.

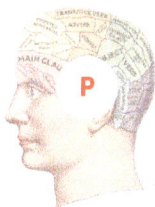

Participle as part of a multi-part verb
Some sentences involve only one verb:

Netta wore a Batman T-shirt.

But others involve several in a row:

Netta was wearing her Batman T-shirt yesterday.

Was = auxiliary verb; wearing = present participle

Netta has been wearing her Batman T-shirt all summer holiday.

Has = auxiliary verb; been = past participle; wearing = present participle

Netta could have worn her other T-shirts, but the Batman T-shirt is her favourite.

Could = auxiliary verb; have = auxiliary verb; worn = past participle

Participle as adjective
Participles can work as adjectives, helping to describe a noun.

The squeaking mouse
The bouncing ball
The broken window
The unsung heroes

Participle as noun
The present participle of a verb can also function as a noun. These are called gerunds.

Swimming is my favourite hobby.
Their comings and goings were fascinating to observe.

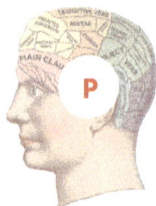

For more information, see GERUND.

Passive voice

see ACTIVE AND PASSIVE VOICE

Possessive determiner

see DETERMINER

Preposition

A preposition is used to show relation between two items. Sometimes, this is physical location:

She's in the station.
He's on the platform.

Some prepositions are used to show temporal relation – that is, to indicate a location in time:

She'll be waiting in the station before her train arrives.
He was standing on the platform after his train had left.
The train leaves at 9.13am.

Some are used to show relationship between two people:

She was waiting on the platform with Magnus.
They sat next to each other on the train.
Magnus was travelling to Salisbury because of his sick mother.

Prepositional phrase
A prepositional phrase indicates relation, as above, but it plays the role of an adverb or adjective in a sentence – that is, it

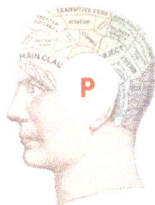

provides more information about the noun or verb.

As an adjective, a prepositional phrase will answer the question "which one?" So:

The cafe on the platform is insanely expensive.

Which cafe is insanely expensive? The one on the platform.

The train after this one goes to Salisbury.

Which train goes to Salisbury? The one after this one.

As an adverb, a prepositional phrase will answer the questions "how?", "when?", "why?" or "where?"

Feeling lavish, I bought a sandwich from the platform cafe.

Where did you buy your sandwich? From the platform cafe.

I'm broke after buying that sandwich.

When are you broke? After buying that expensive sandwich.

My buttocks hurt from three hours on a train.

Why do your buttocks hurt? Because you've been on a train for three hours.
A prepositional phrase is never the subject of a sentence. So the main verb of the sentence will always refer back to the subject that preceded it. For example:
Magnus, along with the other passengers, was relieved when the train arrived.

The multiple passengers of the prepositional phrase "along with the other passengers" are not the subject of the sentence

– Magnus is. So the verb is "was relieved" – referring back to Magnus, on his own – rather than "were relieved".

Opportunity for smugness: some languages, such as Hindi and Urdu, do not have prepositions. Instead, they have postpositions. These serve the same function as prepositions – they indicate relation. But, as the name suggests, instead of coming before the noun, they come after it.

Pronoun

Pronouns – "me", "you", "he", "she", "it", "we", "they" – are used in place of nouns. This avoids ridiculous-sounding repetition:

The astronaut went to the moon. The astronaut performed karaoke on the moon. This was the first time the astronaut had ever tried lunar karaoke.
The astronaut went to the moon. She performed karaoke there. This was the first time she had ever tried lunar karaoke.

Be careful, however: overuse of pronouns can lead to confusion.
The astronaut brought back a piece of moon rock for her sister. She was very happy with her gift.

Does the "she" there refer to the astronaut or her sister? It's impossible to tell. At its worst, this can lead to sentences such as the following:
He fondled his girlfriend's breasts, and then they fell to the floor.

Singular 'they'
There are many grammar authoritarians who assume that it is never correct to use "they" as a gender-neutral pronoun referring to one person. These kinds of people tend to prefer the horrendously clunky form "s/he". There is only one response to these people: Shakespeare did it.

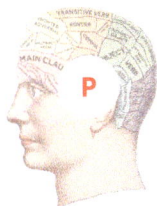

BUT be careful not to use "they" when you actually know the sex of the person being referred to: we have the pronouns "he" and "she" for that purpose.

The astronaut ate their dinner.

This is fine, because you don't want to make any sexist assumptions about the sex of the astronaut.

The winner of the best-actress award ate their dinner.

This is wrong, because it's a fairly safe bet that the winner of the best-actress award is a woman. So she should be eating her dinner.

Subjective pronoun
The pronouns listed above are all subjective pronouns: they're used to replace the subject in a sentence. So:
The astronaut (subject) *waved to her sister* (object)*.*
She (subjective pronoun) *waved to her sister* (object)*.*

Objective pronoun
As the name suggests, objective pronouns are used to replace the object in a sentence. The words "me", "you", "him", "her", "it", "us" and "them" are all objective pronouns. So:

The astronaut waved to her sister.
The astronaut waved to her.
The astronaut's sister and brother both liked moon rock. So she (subject) *gave them* (object) *pieces of moon rock.*

Possessive pronoun
These pronouns – "my", "your", "his", "her", "our", "their" – are used to indicate possession.

The astronaut's sister said, "This is my piece of moon rock." But the astronaut's brother insisted it was his.

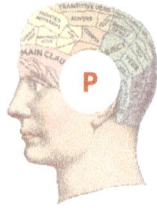

Reflexive pronoun

A reflexive pronoun – "myself", "yourself", "himself", "herself", "ourselves", "yourselves", "themselves" – reflects back to the subject of the sentence. So:

The astronaut was very pleased with herself for buying such good gifts.
"I embarrassed myself at lunar karaoke," the astronaut said.
The astronaut and her co-pilot both embarrassed themselves at lunar karaoke.

Opportunity for smugness: reflexive pronouns should never be used in place of objective pronouns (except in Ireland, where this is common usage). It is not correct to say, for example, "You'll be speaking to myself", or "Can I just ask a few questions of yourself?" People who do this tend to assume that using words with more syllables makes them sound more impressive. In fact, the opposite is true.

Question mark

Is a question mark a handy piece of punctuation that indicates the fact that a sentence is a question? Yes, it is.
However, it should be used only when the entire sentence is a question – usually indicated by the fact that it begins with an interrogatory word, such as "is", "does", "when" or "why".
A sentence that contains a question, but is not a question itself – such as "She wondered why dogs were never green" – does not take a question mark.

Quotation marks

see INVERTED COMMAS

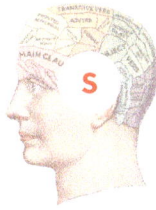

Semicolon

A semicolon links two clauses that would work independently as sentences but are closely related to one another. For example:

There is an elephant in the living room; she's wearing spotted pyjamas.

The pyjamas are being worn by the elephant in the living room, so the two clauses are obviously connected.
It's possible to use a semicolon only if the two clauses on either side of it stand alone as sentences. For example, the following would not be correct:

There is an elephant in the living room; wearing spotted pyjamas.

In that context, you should use a comma:

There is an elephant in the living room, wearing spotted pyjamas.

Semicolons function like a punctuation version of a conjunction. After all, the sentence might equally read:

There is an elephant in the living room and she's wearing spotted pyjamas.

But this is a one-or-the-other situation: the semicolon replaces the conjunction, just as the conjunction renders the semicolon redundant. So what you cannot have is the following:

There is an elephant in the living room; and she's wearing spotted pyjamas.

The other context in which a semicolon is used is when separating items in a list. This can be particularly useful when the individual items in the list include commas. For example:

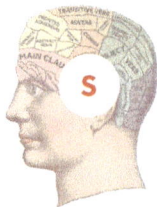

Items the elephant in the living room will need: spotted pyjamas; a toothbrush, elephant-sized; a duvet; a pillow; copious quantities of hay, sugar lumps and apples.

Using semicolons instead of commas to separate the individual items in the list creates clarity; otherwise, you might have found yourself wondering what an elephant-sized is.
These are, by the way, the only correct uses for a semicolon. They are not used to introduce a list (that's a colon), or as some kind of super-charged comma ("No, really pause for breath here"). Used well, they can be graceful and prose-enhancing; used badly, they tend to look like you've closed your eyes, pointed to a random place in the text and said, "Right, I want a semicolon...here."

Sentence

At its most basic level, a sentence is a single clause, containing a subject and a verb. It conveys a statement, a question, an exclamation or a command.

The boy ate.
Did the boy eat?
Boy, eat!

Each of these categories of sentence has a multisyllabic name, thus making it appear more complicated than it actually is.
A sentence that states a fact is a **declarative sentence**:

I am stating a fact, declaratively.

A sentence that asks a question is an **interrogative sentence**:

Are you interrogating me?

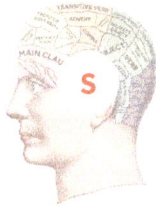

A sentence that makes an exclamation is an **exclamatory sentence**:

Help! I'm being attacked by exclamation marks!

A sentence issuing a command is an **imperative sentence**:

Listen. It is imperative that you understand these rules.

Simple sentence
The simple sentence is, simply, simple. It contains only one clause, and conveys only one idea.

I own a pet elephant.
I'm scared of ghosts.
I like playing chess.

Simple sentences can include compound phrases, as long as they're all within the one clause.

I own an elephant and an iguana.
I'm scared and fascinated by werewolves.
I wouldn't mind playing chess with a ghost.

Compound sentence
A compound sentence links two independent clauses with a conjunction. Each half of the sentence – each clause – could stand on its own, as a simple sentence.
I own an elephant and I own an iguana.
I'm scared of werewolves but I'm fascinated by ghosts.
I have yet to play chess with a ghost, although I once played basketball with a werewolf.

Complex sentence
A complex sentence also contains two clauses. In this case, however, only one of the clauses is an independent clause,

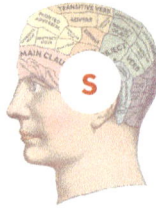

and would stand alone as a sentence. The other clause is a subordinate clause: without the independent clause for context, it would make no sense. In each of the following examples, the independent clause is in red type.

*I bought the iguana **while on holiday in Spain.***
*You have no idea how much fun it is playing chess with a ghost, **until you try it.***
*I'm scared of werewolves **because they have sharp teeth.***
*I refuse to play chess **without a ghost as a partner.***

Warning: you cannot replace the coordinating conjunction in a compound or complex sentence with a comma. This creates a comma splice, which is evil. (See also COMMA.)

I'm scared of werewolves, they have sharp teeth.
I'm scared of werewolves, I'm fascinated by ghosts.

See? Unadulterated evil.

Serial comma

see COMMA

Simple sentence

see SENTENCE

Speech marks

see INVERTED COMMAS

Split infinitive

see VERB

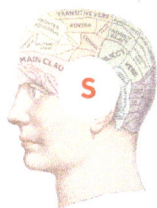

Subject

The subject of a sentence is the person or thing who is doing the main action in that sentence. The main verb in a sentence will always apply to the subject.
This can be easy to work out in some sentences:

The elephant went out to work.

In more complex sentences, however, you might have to think about it a bit longer.

The man wondered what kind of job an elephant could hold down.

It may look like the job-holding elephant is taking on the main action of that sentence. In fact, the main action of that sentence is the act of wondering what kind of jobs elephants can hold. And so the subject of the sentence is the man.

Subject complement

see COMPLEMENT

Subjunctive

Generally, the subjunctive is not described as a tense. Instead, it is a mood. It may help, therefore, to think of the subjunctive as a petulant (yet grammatically astute) teenager, storming up to its bedroom. "I hate you," it says, just before it slams the door. "I wish you weren't my real parents. I wish I were dead."
And that is what the subjunctive mood does: it hypothesises situations that do not exist.

I wish I were a millionaire.
If only I were able to scare away all spiders within a 50-mile radius.

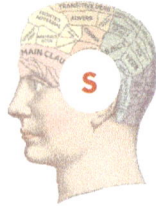

Often, you won't even notice the subjunctive is there: "I wish those spiders weren't here", for example. But look at what it does with the first-person or third-person singular: "I wish I were anywhere other than in this room full of spiders. And I wish my friend Barbara, spider-catcher extraordinaire, were here."

The other time you might notice the subjunctive is in a sentence such as this:

If I kept a pet lizard, it might eat all the spiders.

Technically, this sentence is in the present tense – it should, by rights, read: "If I keep a pet lizard, it might eat all the spiders." But, because you are hypothesising a situation that does not exist, it takes the subjunctive mood. In this case, the subjunctive takes the form of a past-tense verb – "kept" – in a present-tense sentence.

Opportunity for smugness: listen out for song lyrics that completely fail to acknowledge the existence of the subjunctive. *Homeward Bound*, by Simon and Garfunkel, is a good one. "I wish I was homeward bound," Art Garfunkel sings, over and over again. But he doesn't. Or, at least, he shouldn't. He should wish he were homeward bound.

Syndetic list

see ASYNDETIC LIST

Tense

Verbs can be used in a number of tenses, depending on when the event you are describing occurred. To illustrate, let's use the verb "to squeak".

Present simple
I stand on a toy, and the toy squeaks.

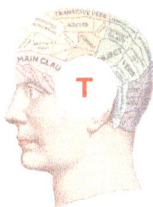

Present continuous
That toy is squeaking. I've taken my foot off it now, so it must be broken.

Present perfect
Look at that gloriously silent toy over there. That toy has squeaked before, and I'm sure it will do it again.

Present perfect continuous
That toy has been squeaking all afternoon. Perhaps it's tired now.

Past simple
Yesterday, that toy squeaked.

Past continuous
All afternoon, that toy was squeaking at me.

Past perfect
The silent toy had squeaked before, so I knew there had to be something wrong with it.

Past perfect continuous
That toy had been squeaking all afternoon, before I put a stop to it by throwing it out the window.

Future simple
The toy will squeak tomorrow.

Future continuous
The toy will be squeaking tomorrow.

Conditional
The toy could squeak tomorrow.

For more on how different forms of verbs combine to create more complex constructions, see PARTICIPLE, MODAL VERB and AUXILIARY VERB.

That/which

see WHICH/THAT

There/their/they're

This entry may sound like it's trying to calm a fractious baby, but it's one of the most important, in terms of creating a good impression. Make a mistake with "there", "their" or "they're", even in haste, and people are likely to make sweeping – and unflattering – assumptions about your levels of literacy.

There
"There" indicates direction: *the best view is over there*.

Their
"Their" indicates something that belongs to more than one person: *the best view is from their bedroom window*.

They're
"They're" is an abbreviation of "they are": the apostrophe replaces the missing "a" of "are". So: *they're going to look at the view from the bedroom window*.

Transitive verb

see VERB

Verb

A verb is an action word. It indicates the vast array of things it is possible to do (to dance; to sit; to tell a lie; to believe; to exist; to

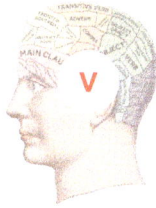

feel). The infinitive of a verb is the version with the word "to" in front: to sleep; to achieve; to pirouette.

A split infinitive is when you insert an adverb into the middle of the infinitive. So: "to blatantly split an infinitive". Or, famously, "to boldly go". The reason this is frowned upon is nothing to do with English at all: it's because infinitives in Latin took the form of a single word – ire, to go; amare, to love – and you can't split a single word. Strict avoidance of the split infinitive can result in very clumsy constructions, so go with what reads best, case by case. Boldly split the infinitive if it is clearer.

To conjugate (another infinitive) a verb is to change its form depending on who or what it applies to: I am; you are; s/he is; we are; you are; they are. Verbs also vary by tense – for example, the present (I am), the past (I was), or the future (I will be). See TENSE for more detail.

MODAL VERB, PARTICIPLE and AUXILIARY VERB are discussed separately.

There are two different types of verbs:

Transitive verb
A transitive verb involves doing an action to someone or something else. In dictionaries, it is often abbreviated as vt. Take, for example, the verb "to pour". You cannot say "I pour" on its own. You pour *something*: "I pour a cup of tea", or "I pour the water". Even if I were a teapot, suddenly and spectacularly endowed with human qualities, I would not say "I pour". (And not just because it's hard to talk with a spout full of tea.) I would pour *myself*. Remember the song:

"Tip me over and pour me out."

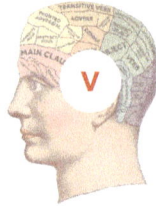

Another example. Imagine the following headline in a newspaper:

Mutant hamsters to take over Earth, scientists tell

On seeing that headline, your first reaction isn't likely to be about the mutant hamsters at all. It's likely to be: "Scientists tell what? Or whom?" (Obviously, you would only ever express surprise or outrage in perfectly grammatical form.) This is because "to tell" is a transitive verb: without someone or something being told, it makes no sense at all.

Opportunity for smugness: try replacing "scientists tell" in the headline above with "scientists warn". That looks acceptable, doesn't it? That's because journalists have taken to using "to warn" as an intransitive verb. In fact, this is wrong: "to warn", like "to tell", is transitive. So those headlines are grammatically incorrect: the scientists ought to be warning someone or something.

Intransitive verb
This is very simple: intransitive verbs are verbs that aren't transitive. They don't need to be done to someone or something. Instead, they stand in their own right.

"To walk", for example, is intransitive. It is perfectly acceptable to say "I walk" or "you walk" without specifying anything more about where you are walking to, what you are walking on, or who you are walking with.
Imagine someone asked you what you were doing. "I'm walking," you might say. Or: "I'm drawing." Or: "I'm drinking." Any verb that allows you to answer this question with "I'm –ing" is intransitive.
In dictionaries, intransitive verbs are often labelled as vi.

THE **tes** LITTLE BOOK OF GRAMMAR

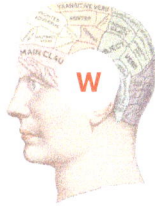

Which/that

People tend to use "which" and "that" interchangeably, but they actually serve quite distinct functions. It's really just a question of memorising the rule.

"That" is used when you are providing information about a noun that is essential to the meaning of the sentence. For example:

The painting that you were admiring cost me £500,000 and a small piece of my soul.

Without "that you were admiring", the sentence would make very little sense: the reader would have no idea which painting the writer was talking about.

"Which", meanwhile, is used when the information being provided is not essential to the context of the sentence. For example:

My favourite painting, which cost me £500,000 and a small piece of my soul, was stolen on Tuesday.

The price of the painting is relevant to the sentence, but it isn't essential: you could remove the clause contained between the commas and the sentence would still make sense.

Another way to phrase this rule is that "which" is used when the information that follows forms a separate clause. Which means that it's fine to use a comma before "which", but never before "that" – if you think you need a comma before "that", you should probably be using "which".

Who/whom

This entire rule is an opportunity for smugness, really: it's not that hard at all, but people assume that it is, so will be very impressed if you use "whom" correctly.

The rule is: use "who" when you're referring to the subject of a sentence, and use "whom" when you're referring to the object of a sentence. It's possible to simplify it even further: as you read a sentence, try answering the question posed by "who" or "whom" with "he" and "she" or "him" and "her". If "he" or "she" fit, use "who"; if "him" or "her" fit, use "whom". So:

Who gave you that rare flying snake?

(Answer: he gave me that rare flying snake.)

From whom did you receive that rare flying snake?

(Answer: I received that rare flying snake from him.)

The man from whom I received the rare flying snake wore a pith helmet.

(Answer to non-question: I received the rare flying snake from him. The rest is detail.)

As a rule: if in doubt, use "who". It is always better to use an informal "who" than to use "whom" incorrectly. The latter just makes you sound pretentious.

Whose/who's

These are two very different words, even though they sound identical.

Whose
"Whose" is used to ask questions about possession and belonging.

Whose feet are the biggest?
Whose pet elephant is on the rampage in my garden?

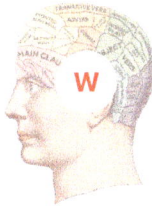

It can also be used to indicate possession.

It's Marek whose feet are the biggest.
This is Peggy, whose elephant is on the rampage in your garden.

Who's

"Who's" is an abbreviation of "who is": the apostrophe replaces the missing "i" of "is".

Who's measuring people's feet, anyway?
This is Peggy, who's the owner of the rampaging elephant.

Your/you're

Your

"Your" indicates second-person possession: this is something that belongs to you.

It's your turn to perform now.
Your prize is three years' supply of prune juice.

You're

"You're" is an abbreviation of "you are": the apostrophe replaces the missing "a".

You're really going to perform an operatic aria?
Thanks to that prize, you're going to be the most regular person I know.

Index

Index

Index

Index

The **tes** little book of
Grammar

Writer
Adi Bloom

Editor
Helen Amass

Sub-editor
Ingrid Curl

Designer
Alex Morgan

"Then you should say what you mean," the March Hare went on.

"I do," Alice hastily replied; "at least-at least I mean what I say-that's the same thing, you know."

"Not the same thing a bit!" said the Hatter. "Why, you might just as well say that 'I see what I eat' is the same thing as 'I eat what I see'!"

"You might just as well say," added the March Hare, "that 'I like what I get' is the same thing as 'I get what I like'!"

"You might just as well say," added the Dormouse, which seemed to be talking in its sleep, "that 'I breathe when I sleep' is the same thing as 'I sleep when I breathe'!"

"It is the same thing with you," said the Hatter.

Lightning Source UK Ltd.
Milton Keynes UK
UKHW020806151021
392216UK00007B/165